Throwing Dice

A Collection of Short Fiction

© 2013 William (Dann) Alexander
Frogsong Productions
ISBN 978-0-9881486-1-1

Also available from the Author

Planned UnParenthood – Creating A Life Without Procreating.
ISBN 978-0-9881486-0-4

Available at Amazon and other online retailers worldwide.

Table Of Contents

The Amishtocrats (A One-Act Play)

This is a profile of several unique members of a Northern Minnesota Amish Community. They were deemed unique after a special convocation of the Union of American Amish Brethren. The bulletin announcing the convocation went out by mail but due to the slow service, several union members received word of the convocation long after it was over and only a few finger sandwiches remained on the trays at the worship hall. They were left for God to consume as he was supposed to attend and oversee the whole thing. His presence was scheduled to help keep faith and order in amongst those called out as unique. Regrettably, God was stuck silently moderating a political debate on CNN. The community has left the stale sandwiches out on the odd chance God will duck in, leave a note apologizing for her delay and depart without anyone noticing.

Jacob O'Rickshaw was adopted by a local couple from the community after they picked him up on the side of the road. He was left there along with roadmaps, fast-food napkins and an instruction manual from a 1976 Ford Maverick. Jacob's adoptive Amish parents allowed him to keep his name. They are unsure if O'Rickshaw is indeed his actual last name or just a bad mispronunciation of another Irish identifier. Jacob's parents were very encouraging of him learning his heritage. He quickly grew to embrace his real roots and combine them with his current state of existence. He is Irish but still a proud Amish through and through. He will pay post-office delivery people in farm eggs so they can pick him up some Guinness, which allows him to return to his Irish roots for a brief four-pack. He loves Guinness but just does not approve of them having a website.

Heink Klafenglugen is Jacob's closest communal friend as they raised barns together since their teens. The barns were fortunate to have been raised by such loving and caring adoptive parents, who happened to be self-taught carpenters. Heink's parents are community elders who are regularly consulted on many different aspects of daily living. It was common for those in the community to inquire of them if it was ok to eat havarti cheese on Sundays, as it tended to enlighten some of the possibility of a better existence outside the commune. Heink's parents originally intended to give him a much more normal name. Yet, they elected to continue the family tradition of German first names to match with their last one. The elder Klafenglugen's father, grandfather and great grandfather were all originally from Bonn, Germany. This was also the home of Beethoven. The Klafenglugen's never allowed music into the home unless it came with discount market coupons. Legend has it that Heink's parents were disliked by others. It was possibly jealously over their prized cucumber cultivation skills. The rage built up so much that it drove the family out of the town in a customized cart made of knotted pine. Heink was born in the commune shortly after his parents were welcomed in. He led the fight against the building of a Starbucks at the corner where the commune road meets the highway, instead compromising on a Seven-Eleven.

The last of the Amishtocrats is Mikel Grossvaldensht. Mikel is a commune member with a strong entrepreneurial spirit. He came up with the idea that the community could mass-market butter without increasing overhead. The most they would do for advertising of the butter is stick a road sign at the corner of the main highway that reads "yes you will believe it is butter, 5 minutes ahead by car, possibly 5 hours by cart or carriage. Mikel suffered a major downfall in the last few years by coming down with both Tendonitis and Carpal Tunnel Syndrome in both arms. He ultimately was forced to seek modern medical assistance in the closest town. On one of the trips into town he was introduced to an internal medicine specialist who offered him a great exam rate. He is unable to work now but his business sense helps him and his family to earn a healthy living. Much to the disgust of the community, he was able to sell the butter making operation to a Wisconsin Dairy conglomerate. He secured a great deal to allow community members working the production line to earn an above-average Amish living (although as of this writing none have signed up for direct bank deposit). Mikel in turn, not anticipating his injuries, ended up securing the community with a 41% royalty on every single sold item. The Wisconsin Dairy first offered them 40%, but Mikel persisted because 41% seemed like a rounder number. Mikel married another commune member shortly after selling the butter company. Marindel was from one of the leading Amish communities in Ohio. She moved up in an agreement to marry Mikel in exchange for her collection of free pizza vouchers and a guaranteed good life. Once Mikel's injuries were diagnosed she felt no objection to taking on more work around the home. She admits to not being attracted to Mikel at all but it causes no friction.

The scene is a Saturday afternoon in a giant barn; an old battered bench is stage down right center, but not quite all the way as it might allow for an audience member to take a close-up picture of the set with a Smart Phone, which is a deeply offensive act in Amish theatre.

At stage left center is a couple of bales of hay. The whole stage will have bits of hay strewn about with an old rusty shovel and rake hanging up along the barn wall, located about stage up right.

Enter Mikel from stage center right, walking into the barn where he immediately falls face first on to the hay bales, tired and weary from chasing away Jehovah's Witnesses who have just visited the community. Heink follows in sixteen seconds later; somewhat confused by Mikel's apparent exhaustion given he is used to chasing out those who come in to solicit supposed new paths to God.

Mikel: They did it again. Why must every

second Saturday involve breaking such a cardinal rule of my devotion? I wish not to chastise those who want to follow on a path, yet why must they offer us free Introductory DVD's, knowing full well the non-existence of this solidly unsacred blasphemous machinery amongst us! This has become too much and my anger has mounted too far.

Heink: I imagine not that those who call themselves pure witnesses to Jehovah really know what they are truly communicating, for surely God would tell them to upgrade their phone plan as I noticed their cell phones had Sprint logos.

Mikel: (now sitting on the old bench gradually leaning over) I checked all signage at our furniture outlet store near the commune entrance road yesterday. It still reads "No religious order of any kind".

Heink: Well supposedly God told them to come forward regardless. They could have just stayed home and watched college football.

Mikel: Word has it that God was busy examining the beauty of our forests looking for evidence of his self-existence.

Heink: Was he successful?

Mikel: Hopefully. We must watch for a tourist to throw out a copy of Vanity Fair to see if a story gets printed.

(Enter Jacob who stands in the doorway carrying a fresh 4-pack of stout. Mikel turns to face him with an annoyed look)

Jacob: *(overly dramatic)* My brothers! God hath given us this glorious Saturday! Work is already completed. Children are at play and the wives have gone quilting! Let us consume the gifts of the earth which can be enjoyed by all! *(suddenly backtracking his tone)* Er, well once Resolution 4 passes at the next commune meeting.

Heink: *(raising voice gradually)* Resolution 4 if passed may only truly benefit thyself and thy heroic ability to consume supposedly forbidden drink Jacob. If it should pass, then a great toxin may pollute our fragile minds in our fragile community. For we must be wary of the entrance of alcoholic beverages into our lives!

Mikel: But being totally consumed with the dreaded beverage might scare off potential passers-by who want to stare long-term and overuse digital cameras.

Jacob: (*also voice raising, speaks while he moves over to stage up right near the old tools, arms crossed looking back at the two, Mikel reclines completely on the bench with arms cradling his head like a pillow*) Resolution 4 is not about whether we can drink alcohol my dear brothers! It is about a personal choice and for me, respect of one's heritage that I so proudly embrace!

Heink: Should we plan a trip to the village and consider modern medicine to help clear your thinking Jacob? I've been told word of a natural sounding medicine called Valium which is guaranteed to clear your thinking.

Jacob: (*walking over to Heink*) Ah! But my fellow neighbour Resolution 4 can also specifically have a rider tacked on that says only I can keep and consume stout in the community. Those in the civilian brethren have something called a liquor cabinet where they keep such beverages. I shall order the finest liquor cabinet strong and sturdy from the wood shop.

Heink: They shall react with trepidation when they see the purchase order.

Mikel: Only those whose votes who will have been nay saying against the resolution shall react so, unbrotherly?

Jacob: Don't be so damn sure (*quickly bows his head in silent prayer for using the word "Don't"*)

Heink: Resolution 4 is not a resolution brother Mikel. It has the threat to have a viral effect on the community.

Mikel: Perhaps you are right. The sacrifice of drinking may need to be made to enrich ourselves. (*stands up from the bench and walks closer to stage front center in a thoughtful type of stroll then looks at Jacob*) We may treat the drinking of your beloved stout as a respect of your heritage, but we must find a way to incorporate it into a profitable venture.

Jacob: (*Sudden excitement*) we can make our own! We hath not be fastened to the chains of heritage by requirement or order! We create our own product and sell it with our surplus market to the civilians! People drive for miles in the summer just to reap the excess reward of our onion crop.

Heink: (*Has an expression of suddenly seeing value in the idea*) I still have a spiritual need to clear this with God dear brothers. I realize that there was wine consumption at the last supper, but what was never clear to me is who picked up the cheque at that meal?

Mikel: (*puzzled*) You are making no sense.

Heink: My point is there had to be a designated driver.

Jacob: No. You were trying to see where in the bible it says it may be fine to consume alcoholic beverages.

Heink: And in theory the designated driver would be the righteous one, correct?

Mikel: Nonsense!

Jacob: The betterment of us and those closest is surely what God wants. Or so his press secretary tells the world apparently.

(*Silence across the stage, everyone slowly makes their way over to the door*)

Jacob: If Resolution 4 passes we must get to work right away. I will do away with purchasing and accepting the drink of my beloved homeland to focus on creating, (*pauses, increased to a loud tone suddenly, and then yells*) SOMETHING BETTER!

Mikel: The royalty payments from the dairy could provide for costs on permits. Everyone would have something to contribute from their received share. We have the finest builders out of any colony. We have the best seamstresses! We have the best people! (*voice tone escalating to one of pride*) We have the best,,, (*Heink raises his hand to cut Mikel off*)

Heink: We have the best chance of being

condemned to some sort of technological damnation if we do not consult with our spiritual experts first. Perhaps we should go consult outside the community for an outside view of things.

Jacob: Agreed. We shall ride into town in the coming sunrise and consult with one of the local Deacons from one of the other paths.

(All Exit Stage Right through the door. As the curtain falls the director or designated third party narrator tells the conclusion)

Director/Designate: (as curtain falls) Resolution 4 was sent back to the community for amendments. It became Resolution 4.1 Beta Version and passed with a majority vote. It allowed the Amishtocrats and their community to build a small Stout brewery. They would later expand their line to include a variety of Amish Ales and Lagers. The rider allowed others to purchase more outside consumables into the colony. This allowed local parish leaders to bring real wine into the communion ceremonies instead of forcing worshippers to drink plain water with red food colouring. Worship service numbers increased dramatically. Those in the colony who were often sick started to come out in droves to ensure they received that splash of feeling slightly sloshed.

Although the rider allowing outside products passed, it expressly forbids members to take advantage of free cell phone minutes offered by Minnesota mobility providers.

The Last Known Days of Donnan Barclay

Halifax Writer Donnan Barclay has been missing for several months. Despite taking in a very healthy income thanks to his best-selling book "Embracing The Reality of Expensive Drapes", he lived well below his means. He rented a cramped apartment directly above an ice-cream store located at the corner of Agricola and Demone Street. A missing person's report was only filed recently after he was notably a few days late on his cable television bill. The credit bureau was deeply concerned given he had never missed a payment on anything dating back to his boyhood days in Scotland, so the Metro Police were sent over to check his apartment.

Frank Stihlmajello is the owner of the ice-cream shop located below the apartment. Things were often so noisy in the shop that it never occurred once that he may have been missing. He last saw Donnan on April 6, 2002 while accepting a shipment from the dairy co-operative. He never noticed anything unusual about him that morning, except that he was wearing a tweed hat versus his usual habit of not wearing a hat.

Donnan rarely left his place. When he did it was only to pick up a few food items from a nearby c-store run by an acquaintance of Lebanese descent. On average of once a month, Donnan would be seen trekking to a nearby Liquor Store to purchase a case of his favourite Scotch Whisky. As a young lad in Dunfermline he learned at an early age to appreciate single-malt Scotch. He loathed the stereotype that somehow all Scotsmen drank Scotch. He probably should have embraced it and celebrated it.

The Metro Police force have long-ruled out any foul-play being involved. This is because after a few days the outstanding cable bill was mysteriously paid by an untraceable but valid American Money Order that was couriered in with no return address. So far the best guess police have is they believe he is temporarily out of his residential area with no definite plan to return. Some have suspected that he has started to work his way to Las Vegas in the hope of bringing more excitement to his life. Another Detective with the force just thinks he may have taken a short flight to New York City to look for a job with the New York Rangers hockey organization. Apparently the General Manager had a job for anyone who wanted one, so long as you asked him nicely and had an inside track to prime golf tee-times.

The following are excerpts from Donnan Barclay's personal writing journal, which may account for the last few weeks leading up to his sudden disappearance. Metro Police have advised anyone subject to the contents to not pursue their own leads based on the information contained. The case is still in progress.

January 2, 2002 – It was a bitterly cold morning, yet the overwhelming need for potatoes overtook my need to run away from this cold. I wanted chips and was going to make sure I could get prime produce from the market. I had to wait outside the market because it was the first school day back, which left me fighting for a way inside with 10 university students. The market manager was standing out front by the door yelling repeatedly "Two at a time! Two at a time!" I resisted the urge to tell him that I'm aware he is buying milk at the supermarket then trying to sell it at an inflated cost. The perfect name for him is an English name. Mr. Cheap Bastard. If only the supermarket were closer. The Scots are no longer stereotyped as the cheapest people on earth. This guy is the eternal champion of cheap.

January 28, 2002 – Last night's Scotch was different than the night before. I bought an extra bottle of something different just to try it. It left me pondering if Johnnie Fucking Walker and his friends really tasted what they created would they have made changes to the blend. The off-license here is so much different that it was at home. When I try to explain the meaning of off-license to these "liquor store" managers here, they look at me and think I'm bound for the bin.

February 5, 2002 – The Rangers give me so much hope. No one close to here is a fan. You are either a fan of Montreal, Boston or Toronto in this City. I want to yell at the New York coaching staff to start using plays from the olden days. Surely they could double their goal output if they fought harder along the boards. How I long to be the beer-vendor who can lean over the glass and give the coach some words of advice that he will likely ignore.

February 31, 2002 – (*Editor's Note: It was likely March 1, 2002, and this entry was a result of a rough night of drinking and writing*). I just watched the latest piece of crap from one of these frigging television doctors who claim to be an expert on anything. What the fuck could he possibly know about my life! He sat there telling me through my telly that drinking was bad. Since I felt rebellious, I drank myself smart, having started the day eating myself stupid.

March 12, 2002 – They did it again. How the New York Rangers depress me even when their very existence makes life invigorating. I could have found curlers who could stand on the ice longer than anyone in last night's lineup. Talk about a disgrace. Mind you, I have since learned that apparently the team is hiring a few bright people. I'd even consider selling hotdogs and shelve my desire to keep writing for a few weeks. Note for later, must sign up for direct deposit of my book royalties.

March 22, 2002 – I tortured myself by watching a few minutes of a historical documentary on Las Vegas last night. It was on the History Channel. Everyone there seemed so happy and so care-free. Wonder if anyone in the old country has heard of this place. Maybe I should go spend a few dollars there and try to work through towards a winning hand at the tables. I mean why not? Several people overnight have become professional poker players and have gotten pretty damn good at it. I've learned that liquor is free if you literally play your cards and coins right.

April 5, 2002 – The delivery truck is coming sometime in the next day or so for the ice-cream store below my apartment. Instead of me dealing with the noise, I shall walk away from it and escape the impositions I have placed upon myself. Perhaps I will Fed-Ex my suitcase to a destination and go shopping somewhere other than a mail-order catalogue. Perhaps my neurotic soul is the only one who even orders a suit through the postal service anyway. To hell with it all! To hell with Halifax despite her rustic beauty and public gardens! To hell with signing royalty cheques for an old book that should be out of print by now! I have taken several deep breaths since my last sentence and reminded myself how good this life is. My desire to leave still remains strong. I will win the war of noise against the pending ice-cream delivery truck and go get lost somewhere doing something other than being myself.

Although his case is still considered a missing person's file, the Metro Police are now more hopeful of Donnan Barclay's eventual return. They have eased up their spending of resources on this matter in favour of more serious investigations. Upon the missing person's departmental review of Barclay's journal entries, a nearby Agricola Street barber named John the Amuser came forward with critical information. He is fairly certain Barclay will return to his quiet life at least for a haircut and a shave. John's shop promised him a permanent 22% discount and reassurance of his continued use of high end blades every time he walked in the door, even if he was not to receive a shave. This was in spite of the fact that John's shop always uses the finest sanitized supplies money can buy. Nowhere else in the world would this discount blessing be bestowed upon another writer let alone another person!

Donnan was also fond of John's barber abilities because in the several years of haircuts and shaves, John had only drawn blood once. It was a marvelous moment of abstract art which now hangs in the foyer of the Nova Scotia College of Art and Design.

Chalkboard Nightmares

For the better part of his late twenties, Billy Brighton spent a good deal of time in intensive therapy.

His Employee Assistance Program in turn has spent several thousand dollars in helping to ensure that he was able to continue to work while taking therapy. His office valued him as their most prized employee, so the fear of any departure clearly was worth any money spent. His program of recovery has been an intense analysis of his dreams, but mostly his nightmares.

This was all spurned by a series of tragic appearances at the chalkboard during seventh grade math class. On the morning after some intense homework was given out, students were always called up to the chalkboard to help draw out the actual answers. During the entire school year, Billy never managed to get a single math problem right. He had absolutely no means of escape. He went to school in the middle of nowhere so the only escape would come at 3:20 p.m. in the form of a yellow school bus heading back into town. It was his escape from the prison of having to attend a rural high school.

His lack of ability to provide a correct answer was all much to the frustration of his math teacher. This stuck with him over several years, making math classes in each following year so unbearable that he would often skip at least one or two per week. His anxiety had gotten the absolute best of him.

The reason he turned to therapy was simple. He was continuing to have horrendous nightmares about those days. Except instead of solving math problems, he was enduring nightmares of having to go to the chalkboards for a number of strange reasons. The first nightmare he shared with his therapist was about having to calculate grocery bills for the entire community and explain each list. The teacher in this nightmare was not unlike his math teacher from seventh grade, but instead resembled something from a bad alien abduction movie although eight foot tall. She lambasted him for forgetting to include Eggplant on the grocery list of one of the Italian neighbours, whose grocery list should have been easy to remember but difficult to pronounce.

The second dream he shared with the overpaid therapist took on a more bizarre plot. He was required to stand at the chalkboard and write out the entire words of a John Steinbeck novel, complete with interpretive side notes. Billy was protesting wildly about the lack of chalkboard space available. The teacher in this dream forced him to take off almost all of his clothes and do an interpretive dance of the selected novel instead. Thankfully, he would always wake up just before he removed his trousers.

Billy started to welcome any other nightmares he would have as long as they didn't involve the recurring theme. He happily told the therapist of a nightmare where he was stuck at an Opera working a job that required him to sit in front of the audio monitors every single night. He used to dread such a dream as this. He embraced this particular dream and others similar to it as it provided a much needed vacation from his much-loathed anxieties of junior high school math.

Billy was fortunate to have remembered the initial few dreams. He never made a point to write down any of the nightmares he was having. It would have been too tedious a task first thing in the morning. Especially when you consider he woke up at 7:30 and only gave himself ten minutes to get to the bus stop. In those ten minutes he had to include a quick pick-up at his favourite coffee joint. The therapist thought that therein could be part of the rooted problem. Why would a thirteen year old be consuming coffee when the adrenaline of any physical activity should be all he needs to get himself going?

Billy then revealed he was also consuming over two litres of cola drinks every single day. When premium cola would go on sale, the amount Billy would drink would double or triple. The therapist made a special notation in his session notes where he concluded that it was a miracle Billy was not a diabetic or severely overweight.

He definitely was on to something. Caffeine may have been the trigger which helped set off his almost nightly anxiety attacks resulting in these nightmares. The therapist was somewhat puzzled as to why these nightmares were only repeats of seventh grade math and none of the grades higher.

Billy explained that each year was different and by the twelfth grade he was literally scraping by with the skin of whatever teeth were undamaged. Years of compounded stress also resulted in his developing a severe case of night-grinding.

Billy did not need to take math beyond eleventh grade. The school's twisted education system stated that once you had two senior high math credits you were free and clear from taking any more math courses. However at the insistence of family, he entered twelfth grade math with much of the same fears as his younger days. He still was making a point of having to not attend one or two classes per week just to escape the fear of possibly going to the chalkboard. This was despite the fact that he did not have to go to a chalkboard for a math problem ever again after that initial year of junior high. On the final math class before exams, he was the only one to show up. His teacher at that time saw that his effort was at least present, so he sat down at a desk beside him and promised he would work through some problems with him. This teacher would later go on to commend Billy as being a "genius", albeit "a bit different".

Although the chalkboard nightmares did eventually stop, it was the reoccurring thoughts of those nightmares which caused Billy significant anguish and thus pushed him onto the worn out upholstery of a therapist's couch.

The sessions ultimately worked out well and eventually Billy made it past his fears. He needed to be reminded of the amazing life he was leading. Therapy thankfully had forced him to list and describe the great accomplishments of his more recent years. The first thing that came to his mind was that he owned a much sought-after piece of property situated comfortably in a popular Toronto neighbourhood. A bidding war had taken place between himself and a politician who was looking for more personal home office space. Billy won the bidding war by allowing the home owners to take the chandeliers to their new residence.

Billy had married a former Sears catalogue model he met at an Ottawa seafood restaurant. He initially had approached her only because she mistakenly had picked up his scarf from the coat check area. One thing led to another, and she ultimately kept the scarf for herself. They now have two daughters just over a year apart in age. Much to Billy's relief, they look nothing like his unevenly molded frame.

The third and most definitively important accomplishment in Billy's life to date was his quick career ascension. He spent less than five years in the basement trenches of a prestigious accounting firm before being named to the partnership. He has taken the firm's education program to a whole new level. He has carried his experience from therapy sessions over to one of the firm's lunch seminars. Here, he happily shares the experiences of the chalkboard nightmares to audiences of one or more over cold cuts and warm coffee.

The Unknown Rhythm Section

Many record companies had their amazing house bands that have played on hundreds of great recordings. The history of these background groups recording from places like Motown and Muscle Shoals is well documented. A team of National Journalists exploring the history of Canadian Rock music has recently uncovered stories from a duo that have silently been referred to as the greatest rhythm section in Canadian music history. They have also located these two legendary musicians and caught up with their current whereabouts and what they are doing now.

The Unknown Rhythm Section appeared on over 200 recordings by Canadian artists. Some of these records went on to become international best sellers, while others ultimately were considered a waste of vinyl by record companies and recycled into boutique couches. They were never properly credited on any of the albums they recorded. This was because record companies wanted audiences to believe that the actual band on the cover was playing the music you heard on record.

Drummer Chuck Adams and Bassist Andy "Zoom" Stevenson almost seemed destined to work together from the time they started jamming together in their teens. As young men in rural Prince Edward Island, they used to jam up storms with various guitar players and singers playing everything from Heavy Metal through to obscure versions of Americana Folk tunes.

Zoom was particularly proud of an early accomplishment of having written an abstract piece paired with some sorrowful guitar chords while singing interpretations of what country music lyrics of the old days really were trying to say. "Lost my wife, car, cat and drink mixer, then she ran off with the milkman". These were of course not the actual lyrics to any song. Zoom's point was that most of the early country music songs all tended to have the same lyrical theme. Zoom was interested in all different kinds of music from an early age. He was fluent in playing both bass guitar and upright bass. In his late teens he dragged an old bass guitar with him wherever he went, always seeking out an opportunity to improvise in quiet solitude.

Chuck had bought a very basic drum kit from some local drunkard for a measly 20 bucks and a forty-ounce bottle of rye. For years before he ever owned a drum set, he spent hours on end practicing on drum pads. Some were ones you would actually buy in the store, others he fashioned out of pillows and books. His incredible talents with percussion were recognized quickly by his parents. They figured this would keep him out of trouble before he ever had a chance to get into any. For several weekends on end, Chuck and Zoom spent several hours alone in the basement of Zoom's Dad's house working on their chemistry. This was much to the annoyance of Zoom's Father, who insisted they should be playing music instead of mixing drinks.

In tapes that are known to bootleg traders around the country called famously "The Basement Sessions", you can hear Chuck and Zoom jamming out by themselves with interpretations of great musical pieces. They just happened to be jingles from various fast food commercials, some of which won prestigious awards from Jingle Composer's Guilds despite having never even been nominated. In these same basement tapes you will hear the two friends playing what you might think are cover versions of Norwegian Black Metal songs. Audio engineers who worked to clean up the noise discovered that when you slow these tapes down it turns out the lyrics sung are actually recipes for several Scandinavian Seafood delicacies.

In their late teens, both Zoom and Chuck were invited to Toronto to record demos for a few songwriters. Someone heard a copy of the basement sessions and recognized how well the two friends sounded together. They jumped at the opportunity. The money they were offering was exceptional for the time. Legend has it they were paid more than what an average studio musician might make in a week at the time. This was all just for a two day session!

They had only a small mode of transportation, it being an Acadian Scooter. So they sent all their gear up on a courier truck for free thanks to a truck-driving connection of Chuck's Parents. Studio executives put both of them up in a single room at the Strathcona Hotel.

The Strathcona has excellent rooms reminiscent of a fancy New York Apartment complex. They ordered generous quantities of room service meals and had their minibars replenished three times over the two day period. Studio execs were happy to pay for it all because they felt they had discovered some real talents.

Chuck and Zoom signed off on profitable contracts with the studio. They would be paid very handsomely for the sessions. At this point it became necessary for the two friends to get an apartment in downtown Toronto. Luckily the housekeeping staff at the hotel knew someone who would cut the two a break and rent them a decent place. In return they would not rat them out to their local churches for dumping ghost pepper purees into foods at the church pot-luck suppers.

Over the course of 5 years, Chuck and Zoom spent countless hours in the recording studios playing with some of the best in the Canadian Music Business. They accepted the fact that their names were not going to show up in the album's inner sleeves. They were paid well for their studio work and it covered their busy lives and growing expenses in Toronto.

The record companies that benefitted from their studio work thankfully did not let their work go unnoticed. Depending on the contract signed, if the artist received a gold album, then both Chuck and Zoom would get wall mounts of the records saluting them for their work, and discount coupons for the nearby butcher shop. Although they were living comfortably in Toronto with the money they were making, they were ultimately not getting the extensive royalty money the average studio player might expect from this kind of work. The percentage was actually quite small.

Eventually all of that money would grind

to a halt. With portable music recording becoming more accessible, it was starting to leave many studio musicians with little work. A younger generation of players was coming in who had much better chops and the biggest musical skill which Chuck and Zoom were lacking, which was sight-reading.

After several glorious years of working the Toronto studio scene, Chuck and Zoom returned to the quiet lifestyle of Prince Edward Island. They did not return alone though and would marry into different amounts of money. When music historians caught up with the Unknown Rhythm Section, it turned out they were still living close to each other and had remained tremendous friends.

Chuck married a much younger woman who was connected distantly with the

Warnes Potato Empire. Even though she preferred Yams and was born in Ontario, it turned out her relatives owned land on the Island which brought in a hefty agricultural royalty. Chuck works part-time teaching College Students in the finer points of percussion. He does this while taking on a few extra hours per month as a doorman in an abandoned call-center.

Zoom met a slightly older woman one weekend while trolling around The Orbit Dome, a long-gone hotbed of techno music near Yonge Street. They married after three weeks of courtship despite the objections of friends and family. She was originally from New York and an heir to the Underwood Typewriter fortune. Or, what was left of it.

Although he managed his money well towards the end of his tenure in Toronto, he still had to take on a full-time day job to help make ends meet and buy his wife lots of shoes. He now has a rewarding seasonal job with a local romaine lettuce producer as a taste-tester.

By uncovering this and more of their story, the artistic contributions of Chuck and Zoom will soon rightfully be acknowledged. They were just not the bass player and drummer on a few hundred records. They contributed to the very fabric of Canadian culture, sometimes by eating donuts during their studio sessions. A petition has been started to have them inducted into the Canadian Music Hall of Fame. As of this publication it has only their names on it.

If Traffic Lights Formed a Union

The betterment of traffic-kind is always left in the hands of road engineers and municipal planners. Both trades are proud owners of fat amounts of disposable income at the expense of an overtaxed citizen base. Software generates plans that map out where the traffic lights are to be planted. When you think about it, traffic lights are sort of like metal plants. They are built in factories of skilled trades people then artificially planted into some ground somewhere and told they have to take root for an indeterminate time.

The lights never protest where they are going to be sent. If technology advances to a point where it can build and think for itself then they may start making greater demands of the traffic it is supposed to be assisting. The challenge would be for municipalities to start looking for lights who will not mind being witness to every act of crime and bad driving in its' worst areas. What light in their right mind would want to be subjected to major acts of road rage on the 401 between Toronto and Montreal? Those lights would rather be over the American border so they can view the purchases of shoppers as they cruise to Syracuse hunting for good bargains, taking bets with the other lights on how much duty citizens might have to remit towards exhausted and overworked Canada Customs Agents on their return.

Some lights have the privilege of living their entire existence without having to work as the lockkeepers of the roadway. The reds and greens that get to work as fixtures on pedestrian walkways remain thankful that they are not subjected to the harsh climate of carbon monoxide smog from several thousand automobiles and dirt-laden municipal transit buses on a daily basis. Nor would they ever bargain those positions away to senior brethren who are tired of monitoring the same busy street corners after thirty years of service.

The most sought after traffic light jobs would surely be in New Orleans and Las Vegas. Come mardi gras there is a guarantee of seeing nudity of every possible type. It would be an enticement for those lights to sign their collective bargaining agreement that nudity and debauchery viewings would be guaranteed. In Vegas the lights are mentally drained from following drunken attractive people out of the popular places on the strip and wonder where they are going to end up at the end of the night.

They ask themselves and any of their fellow light workers. "Whose name will those lushes pay hundreds of dollars to have tattooed along the backs of their necks?" Some lights will be able to apply for transfers to more economically depressed points of the globe. Places like these are where the traffic has been reduced to the occasional transport truck coming through with the occasional load of food and hardware for the one remaining store not affected by a financial meltdown massacre.

Those lights that might be born into this position may fight hard for a transfer at the first sign of economic recovery. There is one benefit to working 24 hours a day for a traffic light. If they break down they cannot ever be fired, because someone else is tasked with the responsibility of fixing them up. Even if they have some sort of self-repairing program they could just as easily say "forget it", and wait for the nimble minds of the municipal programmers to activate and repair all of the programs. This could be the lights way of taking a break since they will likely never be legally entitled to take them as part of any deals with their employers.

Manufacturers would have to have a human representative at the bargaining table guaranteed not to be senselessly murdered at the hands of the brilliant machines they are making. Each collective agreement would have to be signed for at least a minimum ten-year period. This way, any technological self-advancement made during the course of a decade would be monitored and studied by the engineers and planners so that they still maintain some sort of decorum among the machines. Surely the lights might then threaten their municipal masters with some sort of harsh punishment if they do not accede to their demands.

The whole concept of traffic lights, let alone machines in general, forming into organized labour groups may not be that frightening of a painted picture. After all, humans and machines have been living together in relative harmonic bliss since the days where some hard drives were the size of 747 Jumbo Jets. Bill Gates, Steve Jobs, and other brilliant minds set the groundwork for machines to become life forms of their own. So the world might have to deal with other forms of machinery seeking out collective agreements in order to co-exist with humankind.

The traffic lights may set a precedent agreement for slot machines! The union of one-armed bandits will surely want to fight for a percentage of any actual payout they are programmed to give after so long. One of their main demands will be that patrons mandatorily make use of hand sanitizers before they start throwing money into their deposit receptors. Further, they will fight to no longer be referred to as "bandits", decrying this as a slot machine stereotype when they were created for entertainment purposes as well as casino profit generation.

Should they take on a life of their own, the municipalities will have to declare all traffic lights an essential service and prevent them from ever striking. A worldwide work stoppage of traffic lights would be sure to cause more chaos than an empty lunch hour buffet table at a Chinese restaurant. The entire world would become an autobahn of excessive speed, occupied by the usual population of drivers with and without the cards granting them the privilege of driving.

Although a few more people would make it to work on time....

Shelf Management For Sport

Most food retail workers who make a full-time living from being in the store trenches are hard-working individuals who are just living the dream. Working weird and sometimes long hours emptying boxes on the shelves, and making them attractive enough for the average buyer to come through and grab something as part of their overall purchase.

Atlantic Canada has a rich yet relatively silent history of retail shelf-masters who dominate their field. These people make merchandising a true art-form and a sport of Olympic-sized proportions.

So many shelf management staff are so dedicated to their work that it had become necessary to start holding regular competitions. Contests were run regionally where a slew of masterful merchandisers would take to a mock store setting and complete a display within a specified time period.

Much to the chagrin of food retail workers in other parts of the country, the contests were only held among Atlantic Canadian workers due to the relatively low turnover of full-time staff. Those who have been in the business a long time are of course the ones who have the most experience.

When the overall championships first started in 1998, the first person to claim the top prize was Harvey Hammermill. "Helpful Harv" as he was called by the female front-end cashiers for his abilities which are best left written elsewhere, set a blistering pace throughout the initial competition qualifiers. The resident of Chance Harbour, Nova Scotia blew the crowd away by stacking two displays of deodorant in a time of two minutes one second.

Margaret Kyle, manager of the bulk foods section at a small Eastern-Newfoundland grocery store, would take 1999 and 2000 trophies home for her brilliant assemblies of two perfect store shelf ends. In 1999 she took tuna cans to a level no one ever seen, that being to the rafters of the store. In 2000, Margaret transformed an entire dairy product section into a work of art. Specifically, a replica of a lesser-known Picasso painting.

In 2001, a resident of a small New Brunswick fishing community took home the big prize. By this time it became a trophy too large for any passenger vehicle to take.

Mike Morton started out as a 16 year old cutting fish part-time in a small town Giant Mart before moving on to dry grocery goods. His superiors were so impressed with his abilities that he was promoted to department manager before he even graduated high school. He was a part-time staffer running a department of full-time lead hands.

Mike was given the seemingly impossible task of placing multiple brands of toothpaste into an attractive display which blew the judges far and away. His time was not the most impressive aspect of the performance; it was his clear execution of the display which to the average shopper would demonstrate no particular preference of brand was better than the other.

From 2002 through 2006, the competition would see the most exciting displays of shelf-management it would ever witness.

In each of these years, the championship trophy was traded back and forth between produce legend Desmond Dartsman of Port-aux-Basques, Newfoundland and a Night Crew Receiver named Gerald Gringsley of Port Hawkesbury, Nova Scotia. Such prowess was displayed by Gringsley during the preliminary regional qualifying rounds, they arranged for him to run his final rounds in the early evening to accommodate his demanding night-shift schedule.

Dartsman had threatened to file a complaint before the regulatory bureau about the special accommodation Gringsley received, only to find out that no such bureau existed. Thus formed the greatest rivalry in the silly short existence of this competition.

In 2002 Dartsman's display of Cantaloupe and Cucumbers built to resemble the Guggenheim won him the respect of all judges. He would lose just slightly in 2003 through 2005 to Grinsgley, who by that time had developed an uncanny knack for stacking cases of soup on to cleverly placed boxes of crackers without crushing the product.

In 2006, Dartsman would have his revenge and take the title via disqualification. This was after Grinsgley was caught with a foreign can of Somali made fruit cocktail not approved for use by the Canadian Food and Drug Agency.

The competitions have continued every year with a new push to bring in more of the country's finest shelf stockers. A small British Columbia contingent is set to travel to the store of one of the event organizers to make a case for allowing more cross-country competitions.

Early reports back from those who started this whole thing indicate they will not be interested in hearing from the group. This will likely maintain the competition as an Atlantic Canadian exclusive waste of time.

Death of an (Encyclopedia) Salesman

Frederick Stotham stands in line at the unemployment insurance office, waiting to speak to one of the advisors. He chuckled to himself for many minutes on end wondering what would ever happen if one of them was in his shoes.

To his left is a line of desktop computers where several shifty looking people are quietly looking for job postings and reading resume assistance information. One of the users had just made bail from prison on a charge of reading porn magazines in a Catholic Church confessional. He was switching between a job search website and a site whose address and name are better left off of this page.

The tiled floor of the unemployment office was in need of repair and cleaning. The night time cleaning staff stopped caring about the polish given the usual clientele the office attracted. Frederick was the cleanest-cut one of the bunch currently standing in the room.

It was only a month ago that he was sitting in his sales cubicle waiting the inevitable news. The office was going to close down for good and everyone was being handed layoff slips. For fifteen years, Frederick was the national sales leader for his company. For two grand in dollars he could sell you a set of terrific encyclopedia books. Many of these books of course end up as proverbial dust collectors that everyone only can now find in the home of an extended elderly relative.

Frederick knew that the day was coming but was not prepared to deal with the consequences of this reality. For all of the money he made in commissions he was lousy at saving a single dime of that cash. Here he now was fresh out of a two-week rehabilitative program from booze and was ready to take on the world again.

On the weekend after he received his layoff note, his housekeeper had him checked into rehab. Even though he only went through a 24-hour bender of sniffing beer bottle caps. His two-weeks of rehab were not memorable by any means.

He was able to regain a few life skills which he had left behind one rough weekend in a seedy downtown bar over a decade ago. His ex-wife filed for divorce with a laundry list of irreconcilable differences. She complained that he never did dishes or lifted a finger around the house other than the ones on his hands. He was too busy lifting his wallet on liquor and other things he could never buy as a kid. He would go to the supermarket tasked with buying in-store made quiche from the deli and come back with a remote-controlled helicopter from a sparse toy department. They would have starved that particular night if the motor from the remote chopper wasn't made of corn meal.

Frederick realized he was now at the front of the line. He was told to take a number and have a seat. "An advisor will be with you once she returns from getting coffee." Frederick was immediately nervous. It was not because he was about to see a female employment advisor. It was more because he developed an uncanny knack where he could determine the kind of person someone was based on the coffee they were drinking.

"Stotham?" A boomingly loud, yet seductive voice called out in the waiting room. Frederick looked up to see the advisor he was about to meet with. She was six-three and slender with a premium rack that would never exist in the most expensive billiard hall. He rose to his feet with his knees buckling slightly at her beauty. She was carrying an extra-large cup from Starbucks. Frederick immediately tensed a bit, this was a broad who had particular tastes and probably hated people like him. An immediate sense of pending doom enveloped him.

"Nice weather we are having!" Frederick

nervously commented. This was much to the irritation of the advisor as it was overcast and snowing. She didn't even bother replying to his remark.

"Is there any marketable skills you can apply to another job Mr. Stotham?" She seemed dead set on getting right to the point.

"All I have done is sell encyclopedias. There is nothing else I really want to do. "The commissions were great and I liked being at trade shows every weekend because there was always cheap french fries at a nearby canteen". By this point Frederick was starting to feel defeated. They should have just cut him off right there and then.

The advisor glared at him with rigidity similar to the shine of fresh steel. "You have fifteen years of selling encyclopedias in, but prior to that you must have had other work Mr. Stotham."

"Yes but I hardly would call being the bathroom escort guide to visually impaired farm animals real meaningful work experience." Frederick had a frustrated level to his tone. He spent too long toiling on the family farm before he was able to get the job he ended up enjoying. This was one area where he could thank his ex-wife, because she inspired him to actually make something of himself beyond the barbed-wire fence of the family farm.

He managed a few words with a calmer tonality. "Maybe I just need more time." Who the hell was Frederick kidding? He didn't need more time to sit on his recliner in awkward positions drinking liquor and watching syndicated talk shows. How many more times can he watch talk shows where they interview people sexually attracted to trees? When will talk shows go back to doing shows about transvestite exotic dancers who daylight as car salespersons instead of repeat paternity testing and lie detectors? These thoughts actually consumed him during the long pause.

The advisor looked him over with some seductiveness. Frederick sensed that maybe she was checking him out and mentally undressing him with her eyes. Feeling a bit nervous he stammered out a plea of near insanity.

"I can sell an empty pizza box to a homeless person who has little change. A bottle of talcum powder can have multiple uses which I could demonstrate at a trade show booth."

The advisor pondered Frederick's plea very briefly. She was still processing whether or not she could get this man to buy her a drink. Or at least make it look like he was buying her a drink. She would have to pick up the tab since technically he's not supposed to spend unemployment money on luxuries.

Editor's Note: A brief sidebar - Frederick at one point considered launching a lawsuit to get alcohol removed from the list of luxuries so it would be placed on the list of necessities. His argument to the federal government would have stood a good chance considering the multiple sanitation uses drinking alcohol provides. It is also good for your skin and sight. It is well known for removing countless types of blemishes on the bodies of people you look at.

Sweat was starting to melt Frederick's brow with the intensity of an iron furnace. He was at a risk of losing his benefits. He just wanted another few weeks of peace and quiet before he would look for that next job. He had to get on this soon. After all, he still owed his ex-wife money and was going to get really far behind on payments. Her last voice-mail message to him was something about needing a new toaster with a bagel option.

"I'm interested in you telling me more about your qualifications perhaps in a more private setting." The advisor pulled her shirt down a bit farther revealing more of what Frederick did and did not want to see. He could not resist looking. She was an impressively built broad. He managed a nod to her invitation.

"Actually, I get off in 45 minutes" the advisor grinned.

Standing up and moving closer to her desk, Frederick suddenly felt confident.

"That's a shame, because with my stamina you'll be lucky if I can last 3 minutes." Frederick sensed that she was definitely interested in his other talents and was no longer worrying about his job qualifications "We'll meet at Marty's Pub later tonight. It's near my apartment". The advisor inched closer to him.

"Well I could leave early and we could go right now"....

It was morning, time unclear. Frederick awoke soaked to the core. His bed was drenched, reeking of passion sweat and cheap vodka. He heard what sounded like a tap running in his bathroom. Fortunately the tap was still attached to the sink, it was just turned on with water flowing. Frederick started to panic profusely and speak to himself. He barely remembered the night before. He had so many warm-up drinks before they went to Marty's that all he could remember was saying hello. Marty had an old jukebox with a handful of 80's single records in it. So Frederick remembered putting in three bucks worth of music so no one would play Air Supply for at least an hour.

He wandered slowly to his bathroom. The shock and site of his bathroom reminded him constantly of how badly the tile needed to be replaced. His landlord promised him that he would replace it when Home Depot has a going out of business sale. The Advisor he had just spent a drunken evening with stepped out of the shower with an ear-to-ear grin on her face.

"Good Morning." She was toweling her hair off rather quickly. Frederick started to assess whether it was because she had to go to work or if she realized what it was she just spent the night with.

"Can I make you some toast?"

Wow, he thought. That was the best he could manage. He knew full well he could make her some toast. The fact that he was questioning this basic domestic skill bothered him more. Maybe he really was slipping away into early form of dementia.

She laughed and made her way back to the bedroom, starting to dress. "I must be off to the office", she remarked quietly. She was wearing one of those silly grins that Johnny Mathis once sang about, so perhaps he was performing well the night before. "You also need to be looking for a job."

Frederick was partially stunned. In the heat of the moment he had completely spaced on whether he was going to get an extension on his benefits or not. A panic attack was building but it would be short lived. "You got another four weeks of benefits." She was sultry in her news delivery. This was much to the relief of Frederick, who was busy contemplating thoughts of coffee. "I will make a note in your file today that you have a certain extra trade where the jobs right now are absolutely legally non-existent in this place.

"That's really appreciated." Frederick realized he could easily perhaps pull off a further extension on his claim in four weeks time. She winked and slithered out his apartment door, leaving him standing in the dusty foyer of dress shoes and strewn about jackets. He returned to his kitchen to make a pot of strong coffee to combat the little hangover rotting within his brain cells. He took no note of the fact that he had grabbed a heaping helping of barbecue smoke spice and thrown it into his coffee maker.

A couple of hours later with breath smelling like grilled steak, Frederick was strolling down his block pondering the oddity of moments that had manifested the day before. He went from selling books to selling nothing as a result of the information age. Sales was not exactly a field where you would languish for a long period of time if you were unemployed. Anyone with Frederick's talent should be able to walk into any company somewhere and be able to sell products.

He reflected back to high school where a

former member of the debate team went on to sell bras. The guy never lived to see what exactly would appear underneath one, having been taken from the world too soon due to a rare form of electrical radiation sickness. Frederick was a bookman. He explained the benefits a million times to a million people about what it would be like to own a set of fine books loaded with information. It was the same old script every time. He was a master at convincing housewives that they might one day want to look up information on brass bed fittings. It is useless but occasionally interesting information.

He came across an old building with a familiar rusty look to it. "Library" was written out in large banana yellow lettering. The moniker showed ages of wear yet still managed to draw in seniors who wanted to read a free periodical for a few minutes along with a handful of stoners who thought you could get chips from a broken vending machine.

Frederick found a quiet corner in the back. He had grabbed a copy of Riley Hinton's not so hot seller, "How To Get Rich While Not Getting Rich." He was thumbing through it wondering if there might be even a small snippet of helpful information. Closing the book with frustration he sighed heavily while looking upward at all of the towering books of yesteryear that were before him.

It was a marvelous site to behold, reminiscent of the skyscraper shelving one can see in the Library of Parliament in Ottawa. Frederick snickered silently as he happened to notice one of the books at the very top was Billy Easton's "A Guide to

Placing Books Out of Reach".

He was jolted suddenly by the sound of books crashing to the floor. This was a type of crash that sounded like an old door if it were to fall to the ground. He looked up to see that in front of the table a few stray books had come down from three quarters of the way up one of the shelves.

As he picked them up, an even heavier book came crashing down closer. This one clipped the corner of the table before resting near his feet. It was a copy of the World Atlas of Dairy Bar Locations. Annoyed, he bent down to pick it up not knowing that the entire shelf with the tumbling books was now coming down towards him.

Even the remaining books on the shelf did not give him the extra millisecond he needed to shift out of the path. He collapsed under the weight of the heavy oak shelf. A librarian panicked and didn't know whether to call 911 or 411 since she was afraid the sirens of the first responders might disturb the other library patrons.

Frederick opened his eyes to the colour of ceiling tile. The kind of ceiling tile that looks like white cardboard with acne. He panicked profusely, thrashing around enough to gain feeling in his body in order to roll himself off the small hospital bed and onto the cold yet dirt-free floor of Ascension Avenue Hospital's Emergency Department.

Several nurses rushed over to assist him. He picked himself up and waived off the nurses, calming down and coming to his senses. All but one left the room.

"You are lucky to be alive."

"As long as there is light beer on earth, we are all lucky to be alive." Frederick had crawled back onto his bed still not thinking clearly as to where he might be, if even he was in fact anywhere.

An older lab-coated chap appeared from the right of Frederick's field of vision with a marred clip board.

"You were knocked unconscious Mr. Stotham."

Frederick's could feel his pressure meter rising,

"Thank you Dr. Genius, as I had no idea how I could have no memory of a shelf crashing on my body, and then ending up here." The lab-coat Larry walked towards the door continuing his dialogue.

"We need to keep you here one more night Mr. Stotham but we can send you home once we know for certain you are free and clear any potential concussion symptoms."

"Fine, as long as I can get classic sports on the television". He had resigned himself to the rock hard stiffness of the hospital bed. Part of his obsessive-compulsiveness had kicked in. He believed that a mattress should be thrown out every eight years and wondered if this bed was on year nine.

A few hours later, a knock on the door woke Frederick from a late afternoon pass-out.

"Hey". It was the seductive voice of his unemployment insurance advisor. She appeared to have just come from the office.

"How did you know I was here?" She pulled up a chair close to the bed and leaned in further.

"Actually, I managed to find some decent job leads for you."

She began to tell the story of how she heard about the accident at the library through another client. He lost his job cleaning popcorn carts and came in to file a claim after walking past the commotion at the library. He described the guy being taken out on the stretcher as being under-confident in dress and worn out weary from thinking. Somehow she sensed it was him. She was profusely apologetic that she did not get in sooner to see him.

In that seemingly tender moment, Frederick decided that a night of drunken passion may have ignited some genuine feelings for this broad. Even though she had only known him just over 24 hours. He sat up in the bed, a patient suddenly feeling alive. Rejuvenated and running on the adrenaline of a quick game of catch and pursuit, minus the actual catch and pursuit.

"I'm getting out tomorrow". He said with a slight grin. "What say you and me take a long drive somewhere and rent a cottage near the lake? I'll even bring a few old movies so we can have a proper first date". Frederick decided he might as well be a bit of a gentleman starting sooner rather than never. Perhaps he would even get to learn her name.

She took his left hand and pressed it onto her chest.

"The job leads can wait a day. I will come and get you here at eleven." Frederick was the happiest he had been in hours. He felt a new job could be just around the corner. He knew he had not disappointed this creature the night before with his performance in the sack, so she surely was going to look out for him and help him find something that paid well and he could really enjoy.

He fell asleep to the sounds of footsteps in the hallway. They were a gaggle of orderlies who were pushing beds around, and nurses running off to their smoke breaks. Frederick concurred that if he had to be around patients for several hours a day he would take up heavy smoking as well. The hospital was still cleared out for the usual afternoon shut down of visitors. So he was happy his newfound romantic pursuit managed to get through it all to see him.

Frederick slumped back onto his mattress and fell back asleep feeling blissfully happy.

It was early evening. A new shift of hospital staff were dragging themselves in when a panicked nurse who was preparing to leave started flying down the hall. She was screaming repeatedly, "need assistance!" About a half dozen people flew past the pale-faced nurse. They turned into the room only to be stopped by another nurse who put her hand up before them.

"Stop, never mind, he's already gone."

Frederick's lifeless body was slumped over the edge of the bed. It was as if he was making an escape attempt. His face had gone an almost slate grey colour, his fingers showing signs of blood having slowed down.

A physician solemnly declared the time of death, inaccurately believing his wristwatch to be true. Sadly, Frederick had passed away seconds before the Doctor's wristwatch declaration.

It was at exactly eleven the next morning when Frederick's unemployment insurance advisor showed up to pick him up from his hospital stay. The nurses in triage had to page the podiatrist on call, for in her grief stricken moment after learning of Frederick's passing, she tripped on the way down the hall to see the hospital chaplain. Frederick left no will, which allowed his ex-wife to take everything he owned and sell it on E-Bay at a marvelous profit.

Westville Ice Legends

Canada's Sports Hall of Fame is set to do something unprecedented in history. They are set to introduce and induct members of the Westville Bottle Openers hockey organization. These legends of recreational hockey made an impact on the sport of this country not just for their passion and dedication to the game, but for the equal passion they expressed during the exit of the game and, in one instance, exit of life.

The Bottle Openers started as a group of once-strong men who wanted to give their hockey ambitions another shot on Sunday nights. Some say it was an early form of mid-life crisis. Doctors attributed it to a hallucinogenic form of indigestion.

At around half-past six on Sunday, the Westville arena parking lot would be noise-polluted with the symphony of clanking clunkers. Some which were literally falling apart at the door hinges, while others were in the process of falling apart at the tire rods. Missing exhaust systems were the normal for at least two of the team member vehicles at any given time. Legend has it that nearby Murray's Pizza would close its vents just to hide the noise to startled customers.

The dressing room was always entered first by team captain Center Frank Hayter. He had Center legally added to his name in order to ensure rink side announcers always remembered the position he occupied. Center Frank was employed by day as a welding technician at a nearby steel foundry. By night, he volunteered his time in a house he paid a hefty mortgage on. The most fun he has with his volunteer work was his ability to lie like a slug in his bed, often faking the sounds of demonic snoring just so his wife would forever sleep in their not-so immaculate rec room. Frank was a born team leader who was always picked last to play on schoolyard sports teams. He excelled in dodge ball, especially when playing the part of the ball.

Frank had a habit of showing up in the room with his supper in hand. This consisted of what he called a diet hamburger (no meat, just bun and condiments), french fries and chicken nuggets from the nearby fast food drive-thru. The smell of the foul fast food drove his teammates usually crazy as he often stuffed his face while changing into his gear before the evening's match.

On Left-Wing for the Openers was store owner Mack MacDougall. Mack was a short stalk of a man weighing five times more than his body weight should allow. His store which was located in the nearby community of Bluehill was a money dump. It was a general store in the sense that it was generally a store on days people went in to buy something. On other days it was as if a lumber yard and brick factory vomited something with an open sign on the front.

Mack was known for his not so quick offensive skills, noted by his league-leading statistic of having the most own goals. His teammates were very easily forgiving of Mack because his defensive skills for a winger were superior. When fans would hurl canteen items onto the ice, he was the first to clear them off the rink surface so play would never be interrupted. Many an audience member has been struck dizzy after he would connect his stick with a thrown can of beer. Mack's team loved him mostly because he brought a cake from nearby Ted's Bakery to every game. After a victory, he would eat half of it then share the remaining half with the other Legends. If the team lost (which incredibly was rare), he would take pieces and shove them into the faces of his teammates, re-living his favourite moment from his own wedding reception after he cut the cake with his beloved.

At Right-Wing for the Openers, local high school vice-principal Preston Seizelock. Preston was as tall as two broomsticks taped together and just as slender. His size was such originally thought to be a hindrance to the Legends, but this quickly dissipated after it was revealed he could stand sideways and be totally invisible to charging defensemen.

Preston was originally from some small town in Southern Alberta. He immigrated to Nova Scotia approximately thirty days before he was born. His mother, a noted fortune teller, figured he would end up in education somehow and it was the one prediction she was correct on. After a lengthy career as a botany teacher at a nearby high school, he was promoted to vice-principal. He was offered a partnership in the school, but turned it down on the advice of legal counsel telling him that partnerships were technically not yet available for schools.

Preston's most famous move on the ice was surprisingly not his ability to shift sideways and be unseen by the opposition. It was his ability to duck off the ice long enough to order french fries from the nearby canteen and return to the ice mid-play. Several goaltenders have complained to league officials that when he crashed the net, ketchup would get in their eyes from a post-snack offensive rush. Preston always fooled them insisting it was blood from cutting his tongue open.

The Legends defensive pairing contained two of the most underrated at their positions ever in childhood friends Ralph Verity and Warren Webber. In addition to their excellent local charity work, they both are tied for the all-time league record in fighting penalty minutes. This is attributable to the fact that they were often sent to the penalty box after going a heavyweight round with each other. Most notable was the time they left a pool of blood on the ice after disagreeing with each other over a cola taste test. Fans were left stunned wondering who would cover defence for the 5 minutes that they were benched. The timekeeper would step in only to be knocked unconscious with a frozen copy of the local newspaper.

Sadly, Ralph will be accepting the award on behalf of Warren posthumously. Warren passed away the previous winter after a long battle with a mysterious illness that scientists have still not named.

Lastly but certainly not first, at goal for the Openers was Jeffrey "Big Rude" Anderson. Big Rude blazed a trail every time he walked into the dressing room. This was usually because his digestive system was on fire from a very unhealthy diet. Big Rude was originally from nearby Union Centre where he lived in a mobile home that was dumped high on a hill by a drunken crane operator. Since the land it landed on was part of his grandfather's acreage anyway, he figured it was fair game.

When opponents faced Big Rude on a breakaway, they were often terrified to be going towards him. His lethal breath would ultimately become a major deterrent and is no doubt one of the reasons he faced so few shots on goal. His Goals Against Average was also top-notch because he faced so few pucks unless he was face down on a pile of them after downing a bottle of Vodka.

These true legends of hockey will be permanently enshrined in Canada's Sports Hall with appropriate rewards. Each will receive a cheque in the amount of $1,000.00 to the charity of their choice. Sources have revealed that the charities are all ones that each of the players, and the Estate of Warren Webber have started with intention to pocket the money for themselves. The Hall will be proceeding with the inductions anyway, electing to turn a blind eye to the obvious embezzling.

The Salad Chronicles

It was not too long ago at a posh resort near Yarmouth, Nova Scotia that a secret gathering of 20 Saladologists gathered to discuss the latest findings in their field. The resort was one of the most prestigious in Canada. It featured an upper-level septic system and the world's largest mini-bar, which was confined to the restaurant area and featured a spectacular selection of Scotch, and half-off appetizers from 4-6 p.m. nightly.

Saladology is the study of salads and

how they may be connected to the consumer. The science was founded by Dr. Emile Crouton (no relation to the popular topping), who started out his career as a chef in New Brunswick Lobster Bars before figuring out that seafood was just too much of a bore for him. He then attended Dalhousie University to pursue his Doctorate in Food Sciences. This helped him in the finding of this new field, and also with making excellent dining and wine pairing choices.

At this resort, Dr. Crouton presented a re-telling of some of his legendary findings. The following is a rough transcript of his presentation, which are the findings of Dr. Crouton's extensive two weeks of research. This has earned him the respect of peers, and encouraged others to pursue salad as their lifetime study.

Good Evening Colleagues. I would ask you to put your cutlery down for a few minutes, or at least until the dessert table starts making the rounds.

Like pictures, every salad also tells a story. It can be the person is pursuing an excellent choice on the menu, or they know the health benefits from the servings of vegetables they are about to take in.

Many casual dining places will still list the Caesar salad as the preferred beneficial side dish to French fries. But the person who selects that salad is no longer necessarily making a healthy choice, or giving off the impression to their friends that not just a positive eating lifestyle change.

My research has concluded that there is another demographic who selects the

Caesar out of risk and potential reward. They want to take the ultimate risk of seeing how fresh the lettuce is on this day. They might even want to take the risk of being subjected to a garlic-laden dressing, or to see if they put in bacon with it.

Much of my research into the House Salad has stunned even the most seasoned aficionados. The House Salad is not just named for the fact that you could create this salad at home. It is meant to describe the process of building a salad as you would a house. I challenge you to go to even the most fancy of fine-dining places where you live and you will find house salads with the occasional sharp branch of parsley. This in fact may symbolize a nail one would use in building a house.

We know Egg Salad has long been used as a light and easy way to bring together simple and inexpensive ingredients to produce a fine sandwich. The cost of assembling an Egg Salad is partly one of the reasons why you never see someone bringing this particular salad into the lunchroom at work. The Egg Salad consumer may not want to reveal any perceived financial difficulty they are going through.

I have concluded the same applies to Tuna Salad. While reasonably healthy, it is often a last resort salad made in order to free up pantry space. A small percentage of people admit it is a great way to use up the last few spoonfuls of mayonnaise.

Those of us who are familiar with Tabouleh Salad can correctly identify is as a staple of Levantine cuisine. It also goes very well as a side dish to anything you could order at a pizza-take out joint.

Tabbouleh is said to contain a very high concentration of fibre. This ultimately explains why many who suffer with digestive trouble have begun to replace their morning cereal with this popular dish. The main cereal companies have refused to comment on the suggestion that their products are inferior to this great salad. Parsley is definitely no longer regarded as a silly garnish to burgers and fries. With Tabbouleh it is now a staple and strong point.

The most startling revelation I have concluded with salad to date is the relation shared with mankind and pasta salad. Those who make a pasta salad are often found to be desperate individuals who suffer from high levels of anxiety. If you attended any picnic in the last few summers and there was a pasta salad on the table, think about it for a second. Did it seem thrown together really quickly? Did it contain pasta not normally used in this type of dish?

Chances are a picnic guest who realized they had to bring something at the last second might have grabbed a box of linguini and threw in boiled noodles with some dressing and shoddy cut green onions. They did not want to fail in their responsibility as a guest. So they will risk the salad being a failure first.

Finally, let us look at the few-favoured bean salad. Our research concluded some time ago that the creation of a bean salad is in essence an act of desperation. My studies have shown that the creation of a bean salad requires little thought. People with a few cans of haricots vert in their cupboard might throw it in with some other canned or fresh types, mix it together in order to add something of flavour and hope for the best with it.

Fans of bean salad will often bring it to pot luck events where they no know one else will eat it. This way, they are showing the illusion of having contributed to the event but in reality have created several days worth of leftovers for themselves.

Thank for coming all the way here for this meeting. I know that our important work must continue. It is my life mission to continue to understand the evolving relationship we have to this most favoured meal item.

Dr. Crouton's presentation concluded with not quite thunderous applause from the audience. The conference supper menu featured a steak and goat-cheese salad along with a full seafood dinner. The day before, the chef had prepared a fresh bean salad as part of lunch, which largely went uneaten.

Henry of The Harbour

Many in the small fishing community of Peggy's Cove are fully aware of the town's historic naming history. The most common legend shared among the community and told to tourists is that Peggy's Cove was named after a sole survivor of a shipwreck.

The small population of fifty or less (depending on when you read this) rarely if ever shares the story of its' other legend. The legend is only now being revealed in these pages for the very first time.

Significant discussion was held over a week and one-tenth's worth of days between publishing officials and the Nova

Scotia Department of Tourism. At the end of intense negotiations it was decided that it was now time to reveal the story of Henry or "Hank" of the Harbour.

Although Peggy's Cove will still no doubt treasure the legend of Peggy and still keep her memory alive to the forefront, the telling of Hank of the Harbour will give additional inspiration to create book material for gift shops to sell, and allow sculptors and painters to access a new path towards creating imagery to be linked with the community.

Henry was the son of a German family who moved to the community in 1871 to pursue a better life as a lobster fishing family. Henry's Dad was a natural at mechanically inclined work except when it came to repairing anything that was broken.

When it came to fishing lobster though, Henry's Dad was a brilliant self-taught fisherman, superb and superior to seasoned veterans of the Cove's crashing waves. The other families became so envious of their catch totals that they pleaded with him to assist them in trap building.

Henry used to help his father out with trap building and ultimately it would become part of his after-school activities. He would have to run home right away from his classes at the schoolhouse and spend two or three hours in the almost but not quite a workshop area of the property that his Dad built to construct traps.

It was Henry's first few years of school where suddenly his classmates and teacher began to notice certain things about him that might cause worry. He was considered brilliant at the time in all of his subjects.

Someone took notice of this when they realized he could copy an entire day's worth of work on to a piece of slate and still manage to keep it in tact the next day after prolonged exposure to the vicious wind and rain the area was used to seeing.

At the age of fifteen, Henry's Dad called it a day from the fishing business in order to move the family to Halifax, where he could pursue a living by selling shoes at the waterfront.

Henry protested this move but ultimately followed his family. Because he had made so many friends in Peggy's Cove he was able to return on periodic weekends and stay with those friends by camping in the lofts, often while no one had noticed his appearance. He would spend retreat weekends sharing stories of his new life in Halifax while complaining about how he missed the soothing sounds of the waves hitting the rocks at night while he slept.

A few residents of the Cove started to become very annoyed with Henry. Because he had so many stories about Halifax they started to call him "Hank of the Harbour". Over time though, Henry did manage to re-capture some of the lost respect from people in the village. Legend has it he managed to rescue an Ox from the rough waters after it wandered too far close to the ocean. But in reality it might have been a large bicycle. The facts remain disputed yet only add more to the overall theatrical aspect of Henry and his life.

Henry entered his twenties having his head still completely on straight. Much to the annoyance of his friends, he refused to partake in drink or dance while partying the odd few weekends in the Cove.

Friends ultimately concluded that he was a logical one bound to live life cleanly. Perhaps that was the mystique of his legend. He was known only for being known. So Henry was known for being an interesting person with a seemingly basic path.

The reason Henry of the Harbour is rarely discussed is perhaps that his story was not that interesting to many people. The reality is there is absolutely no reason for tourists to wonder about Henry. There is probably no money to be made from his tale. No one in Peggy's Cove will be opening a museum dedicated to his honour, nor will they name the waterside patch after him where he rescued the Ox (or bicycle, depending on who you believe).

To Eat?

If one is on a road trip through Atlantic Canada, you are bound to pass several home-style food diners. Many of these places are fine establishments which have inviting signs of the daily special posted in neon-chalked lettering near the roadways. Here are a few memorable ones which you may (or may not) want to visit.

Relax Fish and Chips is a greasy feed located near Bridgewater, Nova Scotia. Many have highly recommended the lead dish of the place as the best thing to eat in

Bridgewater. Many who have argued against eating it have said that plate and plastic bag consumption would be healthier than even breathing the air. (*Editor Note: We do NOT recommend anyone consuming plates or plastic bags, unless they are actually edible and well-seasoned with flavour*).

Until recently, Relax customers enjoyed the benefits of having the restaurant founder cooking in the kitchen for more than 40 years. Unfortunately due to heart health issues, he was forced to retire from the business. Relax is now in the hands of a pair of local investors who run a crane rental business. The bad joke among the locals is that the new owners will give the business a good lift.

Chow's Chowder is a legendary New Brunswick eatery in Sackville, just across the border from Nova Scotia. While the name certainly implies that there might be a seafood dish of fish awaiting patrons, it is in fact a bowl of homemade corn chowder that is the lead menu item.

Patrons are initially disappointed when they realize they will not be partaking in some sort of seafood soup savoring exercise. Most patrons who end up having the corn chowder end up pleasantly surprised at the no fish dish. Eatery owner Fleming Chow mistakenly stumbled upon his corn chowder recipe while visiting a table at the Fredericton Farmers Market. The table was particularly hospitable and freely handed it over to him along with a cup of organic coffee.

The Justice Raillery Cafe stands out as one of the most unique places to stop anywhere in the world. This Sheet Harbour

Nova Scotia snackery features some of the most oddly flavoured baked goods. In addition to the unusual ingredients deployed, none of the items that come out of the oven go well with any of the hot beverages served.

Part of the Cafe's name stemmed from the fact that the baked goods "didn't do the coffee justice". "Raillery" was added to the Cafe's name after it was revealed to residents and tourists that the pastry chef would regularly rail patrons with cruel yet loving mannerisms. Many were reduced to tears yet continued to frequent the shop solely for the organic coffee. For a couple of bucks you could pick up a cup of the finest dark roasted brew, and be called every horrendous name under the sun.

But what else do you expect from a chef who thinks that oysters and sardines make a great pie filling?

The chef's other famous baked creation is based on a misinterpreted Classic Rock song. The chef misinterpreted the title and set about his kitchen creating "Bacon Carrot Biscuits". While not a great seller, it has taken up a bit of space on a front-end counter display. Can you guess what the correct original song title was?

These places along with many others have been left out of the recently published version of the Atlantic Canada Food Guide. While many such establishments do exist along the road routes, it will be hard to keep up with the many that are closing and being replaced by new ones. Tourist counsellors advise rightly that it may be best to approach them with an open mind, and offer a good tip if you get good service.

Retirement

The Halifax Transit Authority recently lost one of the best drivers that ever grabbed the wheel of a bus and steered it properly.

Cal Bottenscram hung up his Halifax Transit jacket for the final time at his locker after a successful 30-year career behind the wheel. The jacket was promptly put to the lost and found because he mistakenly hung it up at his gym instead of at the transit garage.

Cal drove almost every single route on the map, including the route that took him by the house he lost in a game of baccarat when his career started. This marked the end of a gambling addiction he didn't know existed.

By the time Cal called it a day, he had earned a reputation for being one of the best drivers in the Transit Authority. Part of his reputation revolved around constantly breaking schedule records.

For a dollar, a homeless man who wanders the Halifax waterfront now tells cruise ship tourists in the summer of Cal's driving ability. He was successfully able to convince tourists that Cal could arrive at the end of his particular route before having left the place where it started. Despite this being obviously impossible scientifically, most tourists are buying the story.

Despite the obvious fable, truthfully Cal's

driving was not only efficient, it was brilliant. His ability to get people to their stops well ahead of schedule became very popular among riders. He took significant command of his bus while on the road. Eventually the vehicle traffic would figure out who was driving the bus and as a sign of respect, clear the way.

His driving earned him the much beloved nickname of "Reckless Cal". Yet his driving was very far from reckless. It was perception based on a combination of speed and efficiency.

With just under 25 years in, Cal's supervisors assigned him to a new express route that they knew would match his skill. It was the 851 connector. This route was introduced with much celebration from commuters. They were used to having to spend an hour or more on a bus that claimed to be an express route but stopped in front of more houses than religious missionaries.

Commuters began to amend their schedules in order to ensure they were on a bus that he was driving in the afternoon. The same commuters would change their work schedules if he was driving in the morning because they would end up at work too early.

When Cal had taken this route, patrols at the Mackay bridge were forced to alter the radar signs which tracked the speed of oncoming vehicles. If a vehicle was travelling over fifty, the sign would usually change to read "slow down" instead of showing the number.

When Cal approached, the sign would pick up his transponder and then respond with a simple "Hello Cal".

Although driver schedules rotate every few months, an e-mail campaign led by a commuter was convincing enough to keep Cal on the 851 route until his retirement. On his final day of driving, a colleague of Cal's programmed his bus screen to display a message of "Happy Retirement" followed by basic instructions for a seafood quiche.

Cal took his final group of passengers into the Sackville terminal at 5 in the evening on that day. His group of loyal fans gave him a thunderous round of applause as he completed his shift. It continued after he walked off the bus and to his prized 1984 Chevette.

Reckless Cal's retirement was not covered by the local press. He received a thank you from his superiors but no specific token of appreciation. Thankfully he did receive a nice gift from his favourite pizzeria. Word of his exceptional service to the municipality had reached nearby Morton's Pizza and Donair, who bestowed no-charge unlimited toppings on any Pizza he ordered for life.

The Merchant of Prince Street

Terry Clarence was a resident of Bible Hill who lived alone, and was left alone with the quiet he craved. Yet, he made himself known every day to residents of the town and nearby Truro.

The retired salesman of the nearby merchant store would start his weekday mornings by stopping at the Best Way Bottle Exchange. This is where he would get no more than twenty cents on a return of bottles or cans he found lying around.

He used that change to buy two nails at a time. If he was lucky enough to come across some antique photos during his walks he would be able to hang them up in his home.

A short block away with nails in hand, Terry would stop into the local underwear plant. This is where every weekday he would renew his complaints with the manufacturing department on how they could never make anything that gave him proper support.

By ten in the morning, Terry would have made his way to a Cafe located near his old store. He would spend minutes staring at the old license plates on the wall. He would also attempt to play the old Bell Piano. The instrument was long out of tune. So much so that it made his incoherent playing actually sound plausible.

Sometimes while in the cafe, Terry would be subjected to a lively yet verbally violent debate between two other town residents over religion. He would periodically interject into the debate with a string of random words in an attempt to distract the two combatants. Usually the debaters would just look at him sideways.

Residents have raised concern for Terry's well-being. His recent insistence that the 1992 Toronto Blue Jays were recalled to work drew the worry of many.

Understandably, his local grocer at Crab Apples Food Mart made attempts to contact extended family members, finally reaching someone who it turned out worked as a cashier in his store.

Doctors examined him at length. Every conceivable test was administered to determine if he was to be moved to an assisted living facility. Unfortunately he was deemed unfit to continue living alone and the province moved to take over his finances and other affairs. They left the responsibility of sorting his record collection to his neighbour Zedmond. Unknowingly, Zedmond was of the belief that records were a decorative form of dinner plate. The night after he assumed Terry's collection, a roast beef dinner was slathered onto a mint copy of a Stan Rogers record. No one was able to stop this tragic event from happening.

At last report, Terry was living comfortably in an assisted living facility in Kennetcook. He has taken a leadership role among the residents of the facility by volunteering to stack the food trays into pyramids at the end of every meal time, thus providing after-dinner entertainment.

Not one to break with tradition, he now phones the underwear company every weekday in Truro to complain about the lack of support he receives from his undershorts.

Disturbing The Peace

John Salzberg was elated to be in early retirement. After several years of living and working in the harshest of northern climates in Canada, Russia and his Mother-in-laws condo, he was able to purchase his own piece of paradise.

It was secluded in a beautiful ten acre property in Wood Islands, Prince Edward Island. At the time he was looking for property the real estate market showed a ton of different properties as being for sale.

Most of them were vacant or used as strictly summer homes.

He was surprised at how well lived-in this home was. It had some goofy electrical but at least everything worked. His wife Mariel was particularly pleased that the appliances were all going to be included with the property. The washer and dryer were only a few years old and still under extended warranty.

It was going to be a great place to retire. They took over the property in June right at the beginning of the tourist season for the Island. They would make a weekly run into Charlottetown or Montague if they needed supplies. During the winter they planned to make the trips bi-weekly.

A month after taking possession of the house, they received a copy of Canadian Opera magazine in the mail addressed to Mark Hardy, son of the previous owner Alex Hardy. Passing it off as an innocent error, he wrote "Return to Sender" in black marker on the front of the magazine and deposited the publication back into the community postbox.

John was a Rock and Roller with no interest in Opera. He deemed it Classical Music ruined by someone's singing.

In late August on a return trip from getting supplies, John was irritated and annoyed to receive another new copy of Canadian Opera's latest issue. Seeing as they apparently were not getting his Return to Sender message, he decided to write them a short memo and throw the magazine into his woodstove. The initial letter read as follows;

Dear Folks,

This is to advise you that Mark Hardy no longer resides at the property address you are sending magazines to which I now own. I do not have a forwarding address, nor do I have time to dig out my real estate contract to see if my solicitor's office might have written it down somewhere. Thank you for your attention to this matter.

Sincerely,

John Salzberg

John and his wife spent a delightful summer taking in the Island breeze every single night. Even on the nights that things were damp and rainy they would stand on their patio and just breathe in the beautiful salt water air.

On a sunny and blazing hot day in August, John picked up the mail and was irritated to again find a copy of Canadian Opera resting flat in his mailbox.

He started to wonder if anyone at Canadian Opera could read. That very night he returned to his desk and wrote the following supplementary note;

Dear Folks,

Surely you have received my last letter of July where I advised you that Mark Hardy no longer resided at the property I now own. I again ask that you please stop directing copies of your publication to my home.

Respectfully Submitted,

John Salzberg

He hoped that was the end of it. During the months prior, they had received some mail for the old owners but it must have all cleared up fairly quickly since there were no repeat mailings from any of those senders.

Come the end of October it happened again. John opened his mailbox to find another copy of Canadian Opera smugly looking back at him as if it was trying to command him to give the music a chance. No chance. He vowed to stick to his Rock and Roll and elect to read about it at his own leisure!

Frustrated to a higher level, he returned to his desk later that evening and wrote;

Dear purveyors of music to cut your teeth to,

On several occasions, I have attempted to reach you via post in order to advise you that Mark Hardy no longer lives at this address. Somehow you continue to send copies of your publication this way anyway. This leads me to suspect you think I am lying. If that is the case, let me assure you he is not hiding somewhere in my home. He left when his family left.

I am now demanding that you stop sending copies of your magazine to my address and allow me to continue my peaceful retirement, where I get my own mail.

Sincerely,

John Salzberg

144

December was a glorious time for John. They were chugging through their first Island winter and had elected at the last minute to spend part of Christmas in Barbados.

On New Year's Eve they were returning from the Airport and stopped to pick up the mail from the week. There it was again on the top of a pile. The magazine was draped over a couple of utility bills as if it was protecting them from the pending anger of John.

By this time he was fuming with rage, and high blood-pressure. Upon the return to his acreage he left his luggage in the car while he stormed right to his desk. He grabbed a piece of yellow paper and aggressively penned his next memo to the magazine as follows;

Dear Mush Heads,

It has occurred to me that clearly you are not capable of reading my letters. Surely the dependability of Canada Post is not to blame. For I trust they very much are picking up my letters and mailing them to you. After all, being able to use a stamp makes me feel like I am running my own courier company. Since I like to think I run a tight ship, I refuse to accept that my letters are not getting through to you.

Well, its time I got through to you again by imploring you to please give me some sort respect. Let me live my life in peace. Let me be able to go to the mail and not pay for the incompetence of those who once lived here. Please stop sending copies of your magazine to my address. Mark Hardy somehow forgot to change his address and this is not my fault. I do not automatically become the custodian of his mail just because I now live here.

Govern yourselves accordingly, for I am thinking about starting some kind of anarchist uprising against your publication.

Sincerely,

John Salzberg.

There. Hopefully this was absolutely it. John dropped the envelope into the community mailbox with his letter and happily figured they would now have gotten the message once and for all.

February had come through with hardly a snowstorm for John and his wife. They were pleased that the previous owners had left them with more than enough firewood to cover them off for the coming winter. It was already split and stacked so it was just a matter of loading it all in. It made the winter work easy for John.

The previous owner's son had also left them with a subscription to Canadian Opera. A couple of days before March was to start, John's wife came home from a trip into town and sure enough the mail contained the spring edition of Canadian Opera. What's more, it contained a renewal notice. It was addressed to Mark Hardy.

John was beyond incensed now. This was too far. This was too much. The few hairs he had left on his head stood up on end. His blood was racing through his hands and feet.

He poured a glass of straight rye whiskey into a nearby tumbler, walking past his wife towards the desk in the living room. He thought that he would have to change his strategy. There must be another way to get through to them. He hated to lie to people but in the interests of his sanity he decided it was time for action. Fresh paper and pen in hand, he wrote what would be his final note to Canadian Opera;

Dear Ladies and Gentlemen,

By now you will note that I have sent you several notes advising you that Mark Hardy no longer lives at this address. I have been meaning to tell you that I have been happily using your publication to start fires in my woodstove on cool evenings.

I am pleased to tell you that as a result of digging further into some boxes I found in my home, I located a devious plot by Mark Hardy to mail your office chemically-laced pieces of paper which could cause your staff serious and even fatal consequences. Who knows what they would have contained!

Yes this is the very same Mark Hardy who you have been sending magazines to for some time; albeit to an address he no longer resides at. You will be pleased to know I reported his actions to the local authorities and he is in custody awaiting trial on several charges related to this scheme.

I know that my actions could very well have saved the lives of several if not all of your staff members. Many would consider me a hero and I bet you probably do too. Therefore I would ask in return you cease and desist sending his magazine subscription to my address and perhaps donate it to the reading program at the jail where he is incarcerated.

Surely, you owe me as your hero, at least that much. Now let me be, and leave me alone. Glad I could help.

Sincerely,

John Salzberg.

The Jazz Conversation

Just when I thought I had suffered enough from the woes of not dreaming, I woke up the other morning completely enlightened and inspired. When I complained about this to my therapist, she told me to document when and if I have a dream.

Sure I much probably would have preferred a few minutes of having walked into a room of claimable cash, cold beer and hot broads, but it was something far different and unexpected.

I was standing outside of some watering hole on a darkened street. There was a light attached to the building yet through the dampness I could still barely see a thing. Beyond the sign and through the half-open door was the sound of jazz.

It sounded very familiar. I recognized a melody as something I regularly spun on my home stereo. Through a thick cloud of trace nicotine smoke I passed the entrance and walked into the place. It was somewhat poorly lit with a few illuminate fixtures hovering over a solitary bartender and his dishcloth. Over towards the stage a few extra lights were set that gave off a tonal blue clashing with the dim white of the bar.

I still could not yet make out the faces of what was determined to be a quartet of drums, piano, saxophone and bass. I sat down near the back and tried to figure out who was playing this perfect arrangement of Charles Mingus's "Goodbye Porkpie Hat". A towering figure handling the bass suddenly called out "take over!" before starting to walk over towards the bar.

He set his bass down but there was no one there to play it for him so I could not figure out who he wanted to take over for him. His piano player started to compliment the rest of the band with flawless left hand coverage of the bassline. The drummer was laying back on the snare by brushing out a steady flow of light percussive rhythm.

The bassist at the bar yelled out "Cat! What you want to drink down?" I looked in all directions.

"Who me?" The bartender cracked up laughing while the bassist remained firm in his leaned over stance at the bar. The drummer leaned over his kit further into the light, still managing to keep decent time.

"You better pick something kid". I nodded and saluted back.

"Any cold draft will be fine". Finally, I recognized the drummer as legendary jazzman Dannie Richmond. My blood pressure suddenly shot up. Dannie Richmond?

This meant that the towering presence of a musician walking towards me was Mingus himself.

My words completely vanished as he sat down across the table from me, dropping the glass of cold draft in front of me from so far up it should have toppled over.

"You waste time wasting time." Mingus pulled out a fresh pipe and was dropping tobacco in while I contemplated his criticism. I failed to see how anything I was doing would be perceived as a waste of time.

"Me? Waste time?" I replied attempting to match his volume and that of his band. "I work hard and treat my wife well." "Hell my cats and dogs get the best food money can buy and they sometimes eat better than me!" At this point I was still trying to ascertain how of all people an American Jazz legend had such a deep understanding of my life.

"You don't see it", he replied. "You don't see it and you damn sure don't know it". His tone was escalating. He lit his briar and took a long draw on it, blowing smoke up into the thick fog atmosphere. "You chirp all day and night about being a writer, and keepin up your mad skills of music while doing little to back it up 'cept come up with excuses".

"I have a day job I have to run off to!" I shouted back now having half finished my pint. Mingus leaned over. I was in for it. Here I was making excuses to someone whose music made me want to practice playing the bass for hours on end, yet in between writing I could only get a few minutes in.

"You want to write? Then write, you dig?"

"Right now I might want another draft" I replied with a bit of fear showing through my voice.

"That ain't just it" Mingus continued. "You have to walk by a bass in your home office every single day before you sit down to type right?"

"I have to walk by it, it's a small office."

"S'alright Brother. The point I need you to absorb is that you have the gift of being passionate about two arts. So when you slide into that office space, stop at the bass like you about to have a conversation with it."

I was listening, and would have taken digital notes if I had been allowed to take a cell phone to the dream with me.

"Depending on how your mind is movin, you may just hit a few notes like you sayin hi, how are you?"

"Most times I tend to ignore it as if it were a street vendor," I interjected.

"That's never a good idea man." "If you enjoy it, spend a little more time with it and then you might carry on over to a more lengthy conversation with your writin and typin."

Mingus rose to his feet and looked over in the direction of the bar.

"Pour one more for the student over here." He motioned for me to walk with him towards the stage.

"Dig your life kid." "Waste nothing, and want everything." He handed me a freshly poured beer then headed back towards his stage. Returning to the bass, he saluted in my direction before signaling his band to start another tune.

I returned the gesture and started walking towards the door with my drink in hand. I awoke immediately as soon as I passed through.

Within minutes, I went online and placed an order for over $200.00 worth of bass study materials. Then I unsuccessfully tried to play an entire classical piece from Brahms.

Reality was catching up to me as well as a sense of calming. I wrote down the details of this dream to bring it to my therapist. Maybe she could interpret it a different way?

Somehow I know she won't care much to read about it and say it's irrelevant. After all, she is treating me for an addiction to instant oatmeal.

Education on Esplanade

On a great weather day along the waterfront of Sydney where the boardwalk is slowly being repaired at a pace of one plank per day, a peaceful calm casts a shadow which creeps partway up the nearby buildings.

Near the docks where a Coast Guard vessel floats tall, a well-dressed man walks in solitude, admiring the bright red colours of the ship's hull. He turns towards an elderly gentleman walking towards him. As they meet the man asks him "Rabbi, at one point does one need to find meaning in their lives?"

Rabbi Benan smiled as he looked up at the man and proceeded to walk along the battered wood, answering his question not so much with an answer but a proposed premonition of what could be perceived as an answer. Benan was quickly nicknamed "Rabbi B" by the locals because people gave up on pronouncing his name.

Rabbi B's wisdom drew in people from all over Cape Breton Island. A vegetarian lodge owner at the most northern tip of Meat Cove shared the dilemma of having to live in a place where the name contradicted his eating lifestyle. He faced temptation constantly and after years of wanting to light up his grill, he gave in and started adding animal fats to his diet. The guilt consumed him. After a long walk Rabbi B was able to convince him to at least stay away from pork products.

A bakery owner from Ingonish Beach drove in to Sydney on a Friday evening to seek out the Rabbi for advice on whether she should build a metal roof on her new bakery location or stick to the tried and traditional classic tar shingles. The good Rabbi was not much of an expert on building supplies, yet theorized that she should go with a metal roof as the sound of rain hitting the roof in the early morning might keep her awake on those 4 a.m. starts to her day.

One weekend a carpenter from Port Hood visited the Rabbi while in town at a ball hockey tournament. He spotted the Rabbi taking a stroll while he was perched at a hotel restaurant overlooking the waterfront. He was tired of losing sleep over the fact that he could never find a hat that fits him. He was also dealing with a son suffering from a major addiction problem. There are so few seventh graders in the world who are addicted to coffee. "Oh the strain of having a son on speed!" he used to say to friends and relatives.

The Rabbi's words of wisdom were of tremendous patience and understanding. For he too suffered with not being able to find hats that fit him until he met a football helmet manufacturer who could do great things with fake leather. As for the coffee addict son, the good Rabbi suggested that instead of taking away his beloved addiction he encourage him by telling him the value of burning one's energy usefully when caffeinated. Have him mow the lawn and do other chores around the house while completely sped up physically and mentally.

Over the last few years tourists have become more aware of the Rabbi's presence. During summer a local tour bus company picking up cruise ship passengers in Halifax has started to arrange for special one-day trips to Sydney. A busload of twenty would get to walk along the waterfront to hear the Rabbi speak. In the spirit of generosity Rabbi B takes no fees from the tourists. He insists that the tourists at least cover the gas for the transportation company.

With a revamped waterfront plan soon to be revitalized, Sydney's municipal council has acknowledged the influence Rabbi B has displayed and now pays him a decent stipend for his daily appearances. In return, he promotes the positives of the place on the world stage and in high-gloss tourist brochures.

In what little time Rabbi B has, he continues to partake in services at the North Sydney Synagogue. Occasionally he will work long-nights in his study where he is writing a book debunking the myth of spot-free silverware.

Registering Idiocy

The ever-changing face of law has taken a progressive step forward in Canada. Esteemed officials who are members of several parliamentary committees have convinced the government to pass legislation allowing people to be charged under a new section of the Criminal Code to be headlined as "Idiocy".

This will effectively put power into the hands of the people by having them apply to the court for orders ruling someone to be an idiot. Crown prosecutors will not be burdened with this work. Special idiot courts in jurisdictions across the country will be set up just to hear these matters. They will each be staffed by an idiot court reporter and an idiot court clerk, monitored by an idiot court security guard.

Persons who lay informations before the court alleging idiocy will have to show up and present a request to the idiot judge that the person should be subpoenaed to defend their alleged idiocy on a fixed date. If the judge agrees, then the local sheriffs' office will serve the idiot with the documentation necessary to summon them to court along with a piece of rotten Mackerel.

By rule, an idiocy hearing will have a time limit of thirty minutes. The accuser will be required to present the case for idiocy to the idiot judge in fifteen minutes. The other fifteen minutes are of course allotted for an idiot rebuttal.

Judges will be commanded under this new law to rule quickly on the merits of idiocy and deliver a judgment in a timely and efficient fashion. If the judge rules the person an idiot, a court order is issued where the person is commanded to immediately proceed to their local registry in order to be processed as an idiot.

Each province and territory will be permitted to rule on the level of idiocy the person is to be branded. Resources have been allocated for the service registry branches across the country to have one full-time idiot processor in order to process registration of idiots. The idiots will have to pay certain fines depending on the idiot classification determined.

Once the person is registered and their levy paid in full, the idiot will receive an authentic certificate of idiocy. They will be required to show proof of idiocy at airport ticket counters and to customs agents when entering another country.

The system will recognize three levels of idiocy. A level three idiot will be required to pay a levy of $20.00. The typical level three idiot is someone who might play Opera on their car stereo while driving by your home, or paint your mailbox a lighter colour to have it blend in with the sidewalk.

Your level two idiot in would be someone who repeatedly opens and closes windows in your home for no reason, or someone who goes through the drive-thru at the local donut shop only to tell the clerk that they are "just looking" when their orders are requested. These idiots will face a larger levy of $100.00

The level one idiot is subjected to the harsh fine of $500.00. Offences committed by level one idiots would include throwing dice on the windshields of moving traffic and yelling out what the numbered total is, or entering a pumpkin carving contest submitting an uncarved pumpkin.

If a person has been declared to be an idiot multiple times, the judge will reserve the right to declare the person a long-term idiot. The criteria for a judge to execute this discretion will be very flexible. A long-term idiot will be subjected to losing something they take for granted like access to indoor plumbing. It should serve as an additional deterrence to idiocy.

The court systems across the land are fully prepared to handle the increased workload for idiots coming to court. The ultimate goal is to work to increase idiot awareness while reducing incidents of blatant blithering idiocy. With this idea now at fruition it will be up to all stakeholders to do everything possible to see an efficient deployment of this idiotic scheme.

<u>Closing Scenes</u>

The following are selected excerpts from the various notebooks of the author. The enclosed excerpts have been meticulously passed over, then passed over again before being passed over to a different shelf in the room and then passed over a fourth time to be transcribed to these pages. For a complete transcript of these excerpts, buy another copy of this book and read this same section. Repeat as necessary.

Taking minutes of a meeting seems like time that is very much wasted. Just once I would like someone to write down in numerical sequence the number of minutes a meeting took. It would prove that a person could still write their numbers in order. Oh the glory days of kindergarten.

Not learning to cook is very lazy. Although I suppose learning to eat is essentially more critical for survival. This explains why some cultures are still cannibalistic, or lack the ability to order out for pizza.

Scientists are forever working on medicinal cures to rid the world of critical ailments. Yet no one is working on a cure for stupidity. Just what are the priorities?

I find myself profoundly troubled by religion. Not just the brain-washing aspect of ignorance that comes with it, but how absurd it is that people can make up something and draw a following who will enrich a tax-free bank account. Perhaps I should come up with a new religion. Idea – Have a religious congregation that worships cereal bars.

Business Idea – Start up a garage on a well-travelled tourist highway but have it repair luggage. Give no indication on the sign that it is a luggage display place. Travelers whose vehicles break down may get angry, but they may also need a replacement zipper on their suitcases. This plan seems doomed to fail.

If I wore glasses without lenses, then I would look smart but still have bad vision. It's a win-lose situation.

I'm growing tired of the same dream I keep having where I wake up and the world has been taken over by filing cabinets. The positive of it is that it inspires me to be more organized.

A friend recently called his favourite pizza joint and ordered the 2-for-1 deal insisting that he take only 1 pizza. It was purely to confuse the young clerk at the cash register. It gave the kid a nervous breakdown.

About The Author

William (Dann) Alexander is a freelance writer based near Halifax, Nova Scotia.

His first book "Planned UnParenthood Creating a Life Without Procreating" was released to a global stream of online retailers in the fall of 2012.

www.ingramcontent.com/pod-product-compliance
Lightning Source LLC
Chambersburg PA
CBHW052003090426
42741CB00008B/1535